Tips for Using a Prompted Prayer Journal:

Set a consistent time.
Start with prayer.
Reflect on monthly verses.
Engage with weekly sermon notes.
Respond with gratitude.
Pour out your heart in prayer.
Seek guidance through the Scriptures.
Be open to personal growth.
Review and revisit.
Embrace creativity.

Remember, the purpose of the journal is to deepen your connection with God, foster growth, and capture your faith journey. Stay open, vulnerable, and receptive to God's leading as you engage with your journal.

"For I know the plans I have for you," declares the LORD, "plans to prosper you and not to harm you, plans to give you hope and a future." - Jeremiah 29:11

Shalom

Welcome to the CS Creativess Prayer Sermon Journal for Women, a sacred space where you can embark on a profound journey of prayer, reflection, and spiritual growth. Inspired by the timeless wisdom found within the pages of the Bible, this journal seeks to guide and uplift you as you connect with your faith and draw closer to God.

Within these pages, may you find solace and strength, encouragement and empowerment. As women, we carry within us a unique purpose and calling, beautifully woven into the fabric of God's divine plan. Let this journal serve as a companion on your path, offering guidance and support as you navigate the joys and challenges of life, seeking His guidance and pouring out your heart in prayer.

Just as the Scriptures nourish our souls, may this journal nourish your spiritual journey. With carefully selected Bible verses, thought-provoking prompts, and ample space for reflection, may you discover the profound depth of God's love and grace. Let the words you pen become a testament of your faith, a tangible expression of your heartfelt prayers and conversations with the Divine.

Remember, dear sister, that you are fearfully and wonderfully made, and your voice matters in the Kingdom of God. Your prayers have the power to move mountains, to heal wounds, and to ignite hope. May this journal be a testament to your personal growth, a testament to the transformative work of the Holy Spirit within you.

Embrace this sacred opportunity to deepen your relationship with God, to seek His guidance, and to surrender your fears, hopes, and dreams into His loving hands. As you embark on this journey, trust that He will meet you here, ready to listen, to speak, and to guide you towards a life rooted in faith, purpose, and abundant blessings.

May your prayers be fervent, your heart open, and your spirit uplifted as you embark on this transformative journaling experience. May you be inspired, encouraged, and equipped to live out your faith boldly, shining your light in the world and making a lasting impact for His glory.

May this journal be a treasured companion as you walk alongside God, experiencing His unwavering love and grace each step of the way. Open your heart, pour out your prayers, and allow the words within these pages to become a testament of your faith, a beautiful tapestry woven with love, devotion, and the divine presence.

May your journey be blessed, and may you find abundant joy, peace, and fulfillment in your pursuit of a deeper connection with the Heavenly Father.

Monthly Prayer List

Prayer	Answered

Prayer journal

DATE

TODAY'S PASSAGE   PREACHER   SERMON TOPIC

NOTES

| KEY VERSES |

PRAYER

| KEY POINTS |

| APPLICATION |

Prayer journal

DATE

TODAY'S PASSAGE   PREACHER   SERMON TOPIC

NOTES

| KEY VERSES |

PRAYER

| KEY POINTS |

| APPLICATION |

Prayer journal

DATE

TODAY'S PASSAGE   PREACHER   SERMON TOPIC

NOTES

KEY VERSES

PRAYER

KEY POINTS

APPLICATION

Prayer journal

DATE

TODAY'S PASSAGE   PREACHER   SERMON TOPIC

NOTES

KEY VERSES

PRAYER

KEY POINTS

APPLICATION

Prayer journal

DATE

TODAY'S PASSAGE   PREACHER   SERMON TOPIC

NOTES

KEY VERSES

PRAYER

KEY POINTS

APPLICATION

"Trust in the LORD with all your heart and lean not on your own understanding; in all your ways submit to him, and he will make your paths straight." - Proverbs 3:5-6

Monthly Prayer List

Prayer	Answered

Prayer journal

DATE

TODAY'S PASSAGE   PREACHER   SERMON TOPIC

NOTES

KEY VERSES

PRAYER

KEY POINTS

APPLICATION

Prayer journal

DATE

TODAY'S PASSAGE   PREACHER   SERMON TOPIC

NOTES

| KEY VERSES |

PRAYER

| KEY POINTS |

| APPLICATION |

Prayer journal

DATE

TODAY'S PASSAGE   PREACHER   SERMON TOPIC

NOTES

KEY VERSES

PRAYER

KEY POINTS

APPLICATION

Prayer journal

DATE

TODAY'S PASSAGE   PREACHER   SERMON TOPIC

NOTES

KEY VERSES

PRAYER

KEY POINTS

APPLICATION

Prayer journal

DATE

TODAY'S PASSAGE PREACHER SERMON TOPIC

NOTES

KEY VERSES

PRAYER

KEY POINTS

APPLICATION

"But you, LORD, are a shield around me, my glory, the One who lifts my head high." - Psalm 3:3

"The Lord is my light and my salvation-whom shall I fear? The Lord is the stronghold of my life-of whom shall I be afraid?" - Psalm 27:1

Monthly Prayer List

Prayer	Answered

Prayer journal

DATE

TODAY'S PASSAGE   PREACHER   SERMON TOPIC

NOTES

KEY VERSES

PRAYER

KEY POINTS

APPLICATION

Prayer journal

DATE

TODAY'S PASSAGE   PREACHER   SERMON TOPIC

NOTES

| KEY VERSES |

PRAYER

| KEY POINTS |

| APPLICATION |

Prayer journal

DATE

TODAY'S PASSAGE PREACHER SERMON TOPIC

NOTES

KEY VERSES

PRAYER

KEY POINTS

APPLICATION

Prayer journal

DATE

TODAY'S PASSAGE PREACHER SERMON TOPIC

NOTES

KEY VERSES

PRAYER

KEY POINTS

APPLICATION

Prayer journal

DATE

TODAY'S PASSAGE   PREACHER   SERMON TOPIC

NOTES

| KEY VERSES |

PRAYER

| KEY POINTS |

| APPLICATION |

"The thief comes only to steal and kill and destroy; I have come that they may have life and have it to the full." - John 10:10

"I came that they may have life and have it abundantly." - John 10:10 (ESV)

Monthly Prayer List

Prayer	Answered

Prayer journal

DATE

TODAY'S PASSAGE   PREACHER   SERMON TOPIC

NOTES

PRAYER

KEY VERSES

KEY POINTS

APPLICATION

Prayer journal

DATE

TODAY'S PASSAGE PREACHER SERMON TOPIC

NOTES

KEY VERSES

PRAYER

KEY POINTS

APPLICATION

Prayer journal

DATE

TODAY'S PASSAGE   PREACHER   SERMON TOPIC

NOTES

KEY VERSES

PRAYER

KEY POINTS

APPLICATION

Prayer journal

DATE _____

TODAY'S PASSAGE   PREACHER   SERMON TOPIC

NOTES

| KEY VERSES |

| KEY POINTS |

PRAYER

| APPLICATION |

Prayer journal

DATE _____

TODAY'S PASSAGE   PREACHER   SERMON TOPIC

NOTES

KEY VERSES

KEY POINTS

PRAYER

APPLICATION

"No weapon forged against you will prevail, and you will refute every tongue that accuses you. This is the heritage of the servants of the LORD, and this is their vindication from me," declares the LORD. - Isaiah 54:17

Monthly Prayer List

Prayer	Answered

Prayer journal

DATE

TODAY'S PASSAGE   PREACHER   SERMON TOPIC

NOTES

KEY VERSES

PRAYER

KEY POINTS

APPLICATION

Prayer journal

DATE

TODAY'S PASSAGE   PREACHER   SERMON TOPIC

NOTES

KEY VERSES

PRAYER

KEY POINTS

APPLICATION

Prayer journal

DATE

TODAY'S PASSAGE   PREACHER   SERMON TOPIC

NOTES

| KEY VERSES |

PRAYER

| KEY POINTS |

| APPLICATION |

Prayer journal

DATE

TODAY'S PASSAGE PREACHER SERMON TOPIC

NOTES

KEY VERSES

PRAYER

KEY POINTS

APPLICATION

Prayer journal

DATE

TODAY'S PASSAGE	PREACHER	SERMON TOPIC

NOTES

KEY VERSES

PRAYER

KEY POINTS

APPLICATION

"Finally, be strong in the Lord and in his mighty power. Put on the full armor of God, so that you can take your stand against the devil's schemes." - Ephesians 6:10-11

Monthly Prayer List

Prayer	Answered

Prayer journal

DATE

TODAY'S PASSAGE   PREACHER   SERMON TOPIC

NOTES

| KEY VERSES |

PRAYER

| KEY POINTS |

| APPLICATION |

Prayer journal

DATE

TODAY'S PASSAGE   PREACHER   SERMON TOPIC

NOTES

KEY VERSES

PRAYER

KEY POINTS

APPLICATION

Prayer journal

DATE

TODAY'S PASSAGE   PREACHER   SERMON TOPIC

NOTES

KEY VERSES

KEY POINTS

PRAYER

APPLICATION

Prayer journal

DATE

TODAY'S PASSAGE   PREACHER   SERMON TOPIC

NOTES

| KEY VERSES |

PRAYER

| KEY POINTS |

| APPLICATION |

Prayer journal

DATE

TODAY'S PASSAGE PREACHER SERMON TOPIC

NOTES

KEY VERSES

PRAYER

KEY POINTS

APPLICATION

"For the LORD gives wisdom; from his mouth come knowledge and understanding." - Proverbs 2:6

Prayer List

Prayer	Answered

Prayer journal

DATE

TODAY'S PASSAGE   PREACHER   SERMON TOPIC

NOTES

| KEY VERSES |

PRAYER

| KEY POINTS |

| APPLICATION |

Prayer journal

DATE _____

TODAY'S PASSAGE   PREACHER   SERMON TOPIC

NOTES

| KEY VERSES |

PRAYER

| KEY POINTS |

| APPLICATION |

Prayer journal

DATE

TODAY'S PASSAGE   PREACHER   SERMON TOPIC

NOTES

KEY VERSES

PRAYER

KEY POINTS

APPLICATION

Prayer journal

DATE

TODAY'S PASSAGE   PREACHER   SERMON TOPIC

NOTES

KEY VERSES

PRAYER

KEY POINTS

APPLICATION

Prayer journal

DATE _____

TODAY'S PASSAGE   PREACHER   SERMON TOPIC

NOTES
_____
_____
_____
_____
_____
_____
_____
_____
_____
_____
_____
_____

KEY VERSES

PRAYER
_____
_____
_____
_____
_____
_____
_____

KEY POINTS

_____
_____
_____
_____
_____
_____
_____
_____
_____

APPLICATION

"Teach me your way, LORD, that I may rely on your faithfulness; give me an undivided heart, that I may fear your name." - Psalm 86:11

Monthly Prayer List

Prayer	Answered

Prayer journal

DATE _____

TODAY'S PASSAGE   PREACHER   SERMON TOPIC

NOTES

| KEY VERSES |

PRAYER

| KEY POINTS |

| APPLICATION |

Prayer journal

DATE

TODAY'S PASSAGE　　　PREACHER　　　SERMON TOPIC

NOTES

KEY VERSES

PRAYER

KEY POINTS

APPLICATION

Prayer journal

DATE

TODAY'S PASSAGE   PREACHER   SERMON TOPIC

NOTES

KEY VERSES

PRAYER

KEY POINTS

APPLICATION

Prayer journal

DATE

TODAY'S PASSAGE   PREACHER   SERMON TOPIC

NOTES

KEY VERSES

PRAYER

KEY POINTS

APPLICATION

Prayer journal

DATE

TODAY'S PASSAGE   PREACHER   SERMON TOPIC

NOTES

KEY VERSES

PRAYER

KEY POINTS

APPLICATION

"Commit your way to the LORD; trust in him and he will do this: He will make your righteous reward shine like the dawn, your vindication like the noonday sun." - Psalm 37:5-6

Monthly Prayer List

Prayer	Answered

Prayer journal

DATE

TODAY'S PASSAGE   PREACHER   SERMON TOPIC

NOTES

KEY VERSES

PRAYER

KEY POINTS

APPLICATION

Prayer journal

DATE

TODAY'S PASSAGE   PREACHER   SERMON TOPIC

NOTES

KEY VERSES

PRAYER

KEY POINTS

APPLICATION

Prayer journal

DATE

TODAY'S PASSAGE   PREACHER   SERMON TOPIC

NOTES

PRAYER

KEY VERSES

KEY POINTS

APPLICATION

Prayer journal

DATE _____

TODAY'S PASSAGE _____   PREACHER _____   SERMON TOPIC _____

NOTES

_____
_____
_____
_____
_____
_____
_____
_____
_____
_____

KEY VERSES

PRAYER

_____
_____
_____
_____
_____
_____
_____

KEY POINTS

_____
_____
_____
_____
_____
_____
_____
_____
_____

APPLICATION

Prayer journal

DATE

TODAY'S PASSAGE   PREACHER   SERMON TOPIC

NOTES

KEY VERSES

PRAYER

KEY POINTS

APPLICATION

"Praise the LORD, my soul, and forget not all his benefits."
- Psalm 103:2

"Give thanks in all circumstances; for this is God's will for you in Christ Jesus." - 1 Thessalonians 5:18

Monthly Prayer List

Prayer	Answered

Prayer journal

DATE

TODAY'S PASSAGE   PREACHER   SERMON TOPIC

NOTES

KEY VERSES

PRAYER

KEY POINTS

APPLICATION

Prayer journal

DATE

TODAY'S PASSAGE   PREACHER   SERMON TOPIC

NOTES

KEY VERSES

PRAYER

KEY POINTS

APPLICATION

Prayer journal

DATE

TODAY'S PASSAGEPREACHERSERMON TOPIC

NOTES

KEY VERSES

PRAYER

KEY POINTS

APPLICATION

Prayer journal

DATE

TODAY'S PASSAGE   PREACHER   SERMON TOPIC

NOTES

KEY VERSES

PRAYER

KEY POINTS

APPLICATION

Prayer journal

DATE _____

TODAY'S PASSAGE   PREACHER   SERMON TOPIC

NOTES

| KEY VERSES |

PRAYER

| KEY POINTS |

| APPLICATION |

Prayer journal

DATE

TODAY'S PASSAGE   PREACHER   SERMON TOPIC

NOTES

KEY VERSES

PRAYER

KEY POINTS

APPLICATION

Monthly Prayer List

Prayer	Answered

Prayer journal

DATE

TODAY'S PASSAGE PREACHER SERMON TOPIC

NOTES

KEY VERSES

PRAYER

KEY POINTS

APPLICATION

Prayer journal

DATE

TODAY'S PASSAGE PREACHER SERMON TOPIC

NOTES

KEY VERSES

PRAYER

KEY POINTS

APPLICATION

Prayer journal

DATE

TODAY'S PASSAGE   PREACHER   SERMON TOPIC

NOTES

KEY VERSES

PRAYER

KEY POINTS

APPLICATION

Prayer journal

DATE

TODAY'S PASSAGE   PREACHER   SERMON TOPIC

NOTES

KEY VERSES

PRAYER

KEY POINTS

APPLICATION

Prayer journal

DATE

TODAY'S PASSAGE	PREACHER	SERMON TOPIC

NOTES

KEY VERSES

PRAYER

KEY POINTS

APPLICATION

"But those who hope in the LORD will renew their strength. They will soar on wings like eagles; they will run and not grow weary, they will walk and not be faint." - Isaiah 40:31

Monthly Prayer List

Prayer	Answered

Prayer journal

DATE

TODAY'S PASSAGE   PREACHER   SERMON TOPIC

NOTES

KEY VERSES

PRAYER

KEY POINTS

APPLICATION

Prayer journal

DATE _____

TODAY'S PASSAGE　　　　PREACHER　　　　SERMON TOPIC

NOTES

_____
_____
_____
_____
_____
_____
_____
_____
_____
_____

KEY VERSES

PRAYER

_____
_____
_____
_____
_____
_____
_____
_____

KEY POINTS

_____
_____
_____
_____
_____
_____
_____
_____
_____

APPLICATION

Prayer journal

DATE

TODAY'S PASSAGE   PREACHER   SERMON TOPIC

NOTES

KEY VERSES

PRAYER

KEY POINTS

APPLICATION

Prayer journal

DATE

TODAY'S PASSAGE   PREACHER   SERMON TOPIC

NOTES

KEY VERSES

PRAYER

KEY POINTS

APPLICATION

Prayer journal

DATE

TODAY'S PASSAGE PREACHER SERMON TOPIC

NOTES

| KEY VERSES |

| KEY POINTS |

PRAYER

| APPLICATION |

"Do not be anxious about anything, but in every situation, by prayer and petition, with thanksgiving, present your requests to God." - Philippians 4:6

Monthly Prayer List

Prayer	Answered

Prayer journal

DATE

TODAY'S PASSAGE PREACHER SERMON TOPIC

NOTES

KEY VERSES

PRAYER

KEY POINTS

APPLICATION

Prayer journal

DATE

TODAY'S PASSAGE   PREACHER   SERMON TOPIC

NOTES

KEY VERSES

PRAYER

KEY POINTS

APPLICATION

Prayer journal

DATE

TODAY'S PASSAGE PREACHER SERMON TOPIC

NOTES

KEY VERSES

PRAYER

KEY POINTS

APPLICATION

Prayer journal

DATE

TODAY'S PASSAGE   PREACHER   SERMON TOPIC

NOTES

KEY VERSES

PRAYER

KEY POINTS

APPLICATION

Prayer journal

DATE

TODAY'S PASSAGE   PREACHER   SERMON TOPIC

NOTES

KEY VERSES

PRAYER

KEY POINTS

APPLICATION

"Your word is a lamp for my feet, a light on my path." - Psalm 119:105

"The heart of man plans his way, but the LORD establishes his steps." - Proverbs 16:9

Monthly Prayer List

Prayer	Answered

Prayer journal

DATE

TODAY'S PASSAGE   PREACHER   SERMON TOPIC

NOTES

KEY VERSES

PRAYER

KEY POINTS

APPLICATION

Prayer journal

DATE

TODAY'S PASSAGE PREACHER SERMON TOPIC

NOTES

KEY VERSES

PRAYER

KEY POINTS

APPLICATION

Prayer journal

DATE

TODAY'S PASSAGE   PREACHER   SERMON TOPIC

NOTES

KEY VERSES

PRAYER

KEY POINTS

APPLICATION

Prayer journal

DATE

TODAY'S PASSAGE   PREACHER   SERMON TOPIC

NOTES

PRAYER

KEY VERSES

KEY POINTS

APPLICATION

Prayer journal

DATE

TODAY'S PASSAGE   PREACHER   SERMON TOPIC

NOTES

KEY VERSES

PRAYER

KEY POINTS

APPLICATION

"But the Advocate, the Holy Spirit, whom the Father will send in my name, will teach you all things and will remind you of everything I have said to you." - John 14:26

Monthly Prayer List

Prayer	Answered

Prayer journal

DATE

TODAY'S PASSAGE   PREACHER   SERMON TOPIC

NOTES

KEY VERSES

PRAYER

KEY POINTS

APPLICATION

Prayer journal

DATE

TODAY'S PASSAGE   PREACHER   SERMON TOPIC

NOTES

KEY VERSES

PRAYER

KEY POINTS

APPLICATION

Prayer journal

DATE _____

TODAY'S PASSAGE   PREACHER   SERMON TOPIC

NOTES

KEY VERSES

PRAYER

KEY POINTS

APPLICATION

Prayer journal

DATE

TODAY'S PASSAGE PREACHER SERMON TOPIC

NOTES

KEY VERSES

PRAYER

KEY POINTS

APPLICATION

Prayer journal

DATE _____

TODAY'S PASSAGE   PREACHER   SERMON TOPIC

NOTES

_____
_____
_____
_____
_____
_____
_____
_____
_____
_____

KEY VERSES

PRAYER

_____
_____
_____
_____
_____
_____
_____
_____
_____
_____
_____
_____
_____
_____
_____

KEY POINTS

APPLICATION

"I have told you these things, so that in me you may have peace. In this world, you will have trouble. But take heart! I have overcome the world."
- John 16:33

Monthly Prayer List

Prayer	Answered

Prayer journal

DATE

TODAY'S PASSAGE   PREACHER   SERMON TOPIC

NOTES

KEY VERSES

KEY POINTS

PRAYER

APPLICATION

Prayer journal

DATE

TODAY'S PASSAGE   PREACHER   SERMON TOPIC

NOTES

KEY VERSES

PRAYER

KEY POINTS

APPLICATION

Prayer journal

DATE

TODAY'S PASSAGE   PREACHER   SERMON TOPIC

NOTES

KEY VERSES

PRAYER

KEY POINTS

APPLICATION

Prayer journal

DATE

TODAY'S PASSAGE   PREACHER   SERMON TOPIC

NOTES

KEY VERSES

PRAYER

KEY POINTS

APPLICATION

Prayer journal

DATE

TODAY'S PASSAGE   PREACHER   SERMON TOPIC

NOTES

KEY VERSES

PRAYER

KEY POINTS

APPLICATION

"Let love and faithfulness never leave you; bind them around your neck, write them on the tablet of your heart." - Proverbs 3:3

Monthly Prayer List

Prayer	Answered

Prayer journal

DATE

TODAY'S PASSAGE　　　PREACHER　　　SERMON TOPIC

NOTES

KEY VERSES

PRAYER

KEY POINTS

APPLICATION

Prayer journal

DATE

TODAY'S PASSAGE   PREACHER   SERMON TOPIC

NOTES

KEY VERSES

PRAYER

KEY POINTS

APPLICATION

Prayer journal

DATE

TODAY'S PASSAGE   PREACHER   SERMON TOPIC

NOTES

KEY VERSES

PRAYER

KEY POINTS

APPLICATION

Prayer journal

DATE

TODAY'S PASSAGE   PREACHER   SERMON TOPIC

NOTES

KEY VERSES

PRAYER

KEY POINTS

APPLICATION

Prayer journal

DATE

TODAY'S PASSAGE   PREACHER   SERMON TOPIC

NOTES

| KEY VERSES |

PRAYER

| KEY POINTS |

| APPLICATION |

"Now he who supplies seed to the sower and bread for food will also supply and increase your store of seed and will enlarge the harvest of your righteousness. You will be enriched in every way so that you can be generous on every occasion." - 2 Corinthians 9:10-11

Monthly Prayer List

Prayer	Answered

Prayer journal

DATE

TODAY'S PASSAGE　　PREACHER　　SERMON TOPIC

NOTES

KEY VERSES

PRAYER

KEY POINTS

APPLICATION

Prayer journal

DATE

TODAY'S PASSAGE PREACHER SERMON TOPIC

NOTES

KEY VERSES

PRAYER

KEY POINTS

APPLICATION

Prayer journal

DATE

TODAY'S PASSAGE   PREACHER   SERMON TOPIC

NOTES

KEY VERSES

PRAYER

KEY POINTS

APPLICATION

Prayer journal

DATE

TODAY'S PASSAGE   PREACHER   SERMON TOPIC

NOTES

| KEY VERSES |

PRAYER

| KEY POINTS |

| APPLICATION |

Prayer journal

DATE

TODAY'S PASSAGE　　　PREACHER　　　SERMON TOPIC

NOTES

KEY VERSES

PRAYER

KEY POINTS

APPLICATION

"Many are the plans in a person's heart, but it is the LORD's purpose that prevails." - Proverbs 19:21

Monthly Prayer List

Prayer	Answered

Prayer journal

DATE

TODAY'S PASSAGE   PREACHER   SERMON TOPIC

NOTES

KEY VERSES

PRAYER

KEY POINTS

APPLICATION

Prayer journal

DATE

TODAY'S PASSAGE   PREACHER   SERMON TOPIC

NOTES

KEY VERSES

PRAYER

KEY POINTS

APPLICATION

Prayer journal

DATE

TODAY'S PASSAGE		PREACHER		SERMON TOPIC

NOTES

KEY VERSES

PRAYER

KEY POINTS

APPLICATION

Prayer journal

DATE

TODAY'S PASSAGE   PREACHER   SERMON TOPIC

NOTES

KEY VERSES

PRAYER

KEY POINTS

APPLICATION

Prayer journal

DATE _____

TODAY'S PASSAGE   PREACHER   SERMON TOPIC

NOTES
_____
_____
_____
_____
_____
_____
_____
_____
_____
_____

PRAYER
_____
_____
_____
_____
_____
_____
_____
_____
_____
_____
_____
_____
_____
_____
_____

KEY VERSES

KEY POINTS

APPLICATION

"Charm is deceptive, and beauty is fleeting; but a woman who fears the LORD is to be praised." - Proverbs 31:30

Monthly Prayer List

Prayer	Answered

Prayer journal

DATE _____

TODAY'S PASSAGE   PREACHER   SERMON TOPIC

NOTES

_____
_____
_____
_____
_____
_____
_____
_____
_____
_____
_____

PRAYER

_____
_____
_____
_____
_____
_____
_____
_____
_____
_____
_____
_____
_____
_____
_____

KEY VERSES

KEY POINTS

APPLICATION

Prayer journal

DATE

TODAY'S PASSAGE PREACHER SERMON TOPIC

NOTES

| KEY VERSES |

PRAYER

| KEY POINTS |

| APPLICATION |

Prayer journal

DATE

TODAY'S PASSAGE   PREACHER   SERMON TOPIC

NOTES

KEY VERSES

PRAYER

KEY POINTS

APPLICATION

Prayer journal

DATE: _____

TODAY'S PASSAGE   PREACHER   SERMON TOPIC

NOTES
_____
_____
_____
_____
_____
_____
_____
_____
_____
_____
_____
_____

PRAYER
_____
_____
_____
_____
_____
_____
_____
_____
_____
_____
_____
_____
_____
_____
_____

KEY VERSES

KEY POINTS

APPLICATION

Prayer journal

DATE

TODAY'S PASSAGE   PREACHER   SERMON TOPIC

NOTES

KEY VERSES

PRAYER

KEY POINTS

APPLICATION

"For though we live in the world, we do not wage war as the world does. The weapons we fight with are not the weapons of the world. On the contrary, they have divine power to demolish strongholds." - 2 Corinthians 10:3-4

Monthly Prayer List

Prayer	Answered

Prayer journal

DATE

TODAY'S PASSAGE   PREACHER   SERMON TOPIC

NOTES

KEY VERSES

PRAYER

KEY POINTS

APPLICATION

Prayer journal

DATE

TODAY'S PASSAGE   PREACHER   SERMON TOPIC

NOTES

KEY VERSES

PRAYER

KEY POINTS

APPLICATION

Prayer journal

DATE _____

TODAY'S PASSAGE   PREACHER   SERMON TOPIC

NOTES
_____
_____
_____
_____
_____
_____
_____
_____
_____
_____
_____
_____
_____

PRAYER
_____
_____
_____
_____
_____
_____
_____
_____
_____
_____
_____
_____
_____
_____

KEY VERSES

KEY POINTS

APPLICATION

Prayer journal

DATE

TODAY'S PASSAGE   PREACHER   SERMON TOPIC

NOTES

KEY VERSES

PRAYER

KEY POINTS

APPLICATION

Prayer journal

DATE: _____

TODAY'S PASSAGE   PREACHER   SERMON TOPIC

NOTES

_____
_____
_____
_____
_____
_____
_____
_____
_____
_____

KEY VERSES

PRAYER

_____
_____
_____
_____
_____
_____
_____

KEY POINTS

_____
_____
_____
_____
_____
_____
_____
_____

APPLICATION

"Be still before the LORD and wait patiently for him; do not fret when people succeed in their ways, when they carry out their wicked schemes." - Psalm 37:7

Monthly Prayer List

Prayer	Answered

Prayer journal

DATE

TODAY'S PASSAGE   PREACHER   SERMON TOPIC

NOTES

KEY VERSES

PRAYER

KEY POINTS

APPLICATION

Prayer journal

DATE

TODAY'S PASSAGE   PREACHER   SERMON TOPIC

NOTES

KEY VERSES

PRAYER

KEY POINTS

APPLICATION

Prayer journal

DATE

TODAY'S PASSAGE **PREACHER** **SERMON TOPIC**

NOTES

KEY VERSES

PRAYER

KEY POINTS

APPLICATION

Prayer journal

DATE

TODAY'S PASSAGE   PREACHER   SERMON TOPIC

NOTES

KEY VERSES

PRAYER

KEY POINTS

APPLICATION

Prayer journal

DATE _____

TODAY'S PASSAGE   PREACHER   SERMON TOPIC

NOTES

PRAYER

KEY VERSES

KEY POINTS

APPLICATION

"Give thanks in all circumstances; for this is God's will for you in Christ Jesus." - 1 Thessalonians 5:18

Monthly Prayer List

Prayer	Answered

Prayer journal

DATE _____

TODAY'S PASSAGE   PREACHER   SERMON TOPIC

NOTES

KEY VERSES

KEY POINTS

PRAYER

APPLICATION

Prayer journal

DATE

TODAY'S PASSAGE   PREACHER   SERMON TOPIC

NOTES

KEY VERSES

PRAYER

KEY POINTS

APPLICATION

Prayer journal

DATE

TODAY'S PASSAGE PREACHER SERMON TOPIC

NOTES

KEY VERSES

PRAYER

KEY POINTS

APPLICATION

Prayer journal

DATE

TODAY'S PASSAGE PREACHER SERMON TOPIC

NOTES

KEY VERSES

PRAYER

KEY POINTS

APPLICATION

Prayer journal

DATE

TODAY'S PASSAGE   PREACHER   SERMON TOPIC

NOTES

KEY VERSES

PRAYER

KEY POINTS

APPLICATION

"Be joyful in hope, patient in affliction, faithful in prayer." - Romans 12:12

"I can do all this through him who gives me strength." - Philippians 4:13

Monthly Prayer List

Prayer	Answered

Prayer journal

DATE

TODAY'S PASSAGE   PREACHER   SERMON TOPIC

NOTES

KEY VERSES

PRAYER

KEY POINTS

APPLICATION

Prayer journal

DATE

TODAY'S PASSAGE   PREACHER   SERMON TOPIC

NOTES

KEY VERSES

PRAYER

KEY POINTS

APPLICATION

Prayer journal

DATE

TODAY'S PASSAGE   PREACHER   SERMON TOPIC

NOTES

KEY VERSES

PRAYER

KEY POINTS

APPLICATION

Prayer journal

DATE

TODAY'S PASSAGE　　　PREACHER　　　SERMON TOPIC

NOTES

KEY VERSES

PRAYER

KEY POINTS

APPLICATION

Prayer journal

DATE

TODAY'S PASSAGE　　　PREACHER　　　SERMON TOPIC

NOTES

KEY VERSES

PRAYER

KEY POINTS

APPLICATION

"But those who hope in the LORD will renew their strength. They will soar on wings like eagles; they will run and not grow weary, they will walk and not be faint." - Isaiah 40:31

Monthly Prayer List

Prayer	Answered

Prayer journal

DATE _____

TODAY'S PASSAGE   PREACHER   SERMON TOPIC

NOTES

_____
_____
_____
_____
_____
_____
_____
_____
_____
_____

KEY VERSES

PRAYER

_____
_____
_____
_____
_____
_____
_____
_____
_____
_____
_____
_____
_____
_____
_____
_____

KEY POINTS

APPLICATION

Prayer journal

DATE _____

TODAY'S PASSAGE _____   PREACHER _____   SERMON TOPIC _____

NOTES

_____
_____
_____
_____
_____
_____
_____
_____
_____
_____

PRAYER

_____
_____
_____
_____
_____
_____
_____
_____
_____
_____
_____
_____
_____
_____
_____
_____

KEY VERSES

KEY POINTS

APPLICATION

Prayer journal

DATE

TODAY'S PASSAGE   PREACHER   SERMON TOPIC

NOTES

| KEY VERSES |

PRAYER

| KEY POINTS |

| APPLICATION |

Prayer journal

DATE

TODAY'S PASSAGE   PREACHER   SERMON TOPIC

NOTES

KEY VERSES

PRAYER

KEY POINTS

APPLICATION

Prayer journal

DATE

TODAY'S PASSAGE   PREACHER   SERMON TOPIC

NOTES

KEY VERSES

PRAYER

KEY POINTS

APPLICATION

"If any of you lacks wisdom, you should ask God, who gives generously to all without finding fault, and it will be given to you."
- James 1:5

Monthly Prayer List

Prayer	Answered

Prayer journal

DATE

TODAY'S PASSAGE   PREACHER   SERMON TOPIC

NOTES

KEY VERSES

PRAYER

KEY POINTS

APPLICATION

Prayer journal

DATE

TODAY'S PASSAGE PREACHER SERMON TOPIC

NOTES

KEY VERSES

PRAYER

KEY POINTS

APPLICATION

Prayer journal

DATE

TODAY'S PASSAGE   PREACHER   SERMON TOPIC

NOTES

KEY VERSES

PRAYER

KEY POINTS

APPLICATION

Prayer journal

DATE _____

TODAY'S PASSAGE _____ PREACHER _____ SERMON TOPIC _____

NOTES
_____
_____
_____
_____
_____
_____
_____
_____
_____
_____

KEY VERSES

PRAYER
_____
_____
_____
_____
_____
_____
_____

KEY POINTS

_____
_____
_____
_____
_____
_____
_____
_____

APPLICATION

Prayer journal

DATE

TODAY'S PASSAGE   PREACHER   SERMON TOPIC

NOTES

KEY VERSES

KEY POINTS

PRAYER

APPLICATION

"The LORD is my rock, my fortress, and my deliverer; my God is my rock, in whom I take refuge, my shield and the horn of my salvation, my stronghold." - Psalm 18:2

Monthly Prayer List

Prayer	Answered

Prayer journal

DATE

TODAY'S PASSAGE   PREACHER   SERMON TOPIC

NOTES

KEY VERSES

PRAYER

KEY POINTS

APPLICATION

Prayer journal

DATE

TODAY'S PASSAGE   PREACHER   SERMON TOPIC

NOTES

KEY VERSES

PRAYER

KEY POINTS

APPLICATION

Prayer journal

DATE _____

TODAY'S PASSAGE   PREACHER   SERMON TOPIC

NOTES

_____
_____
_____
_____
_____
_____
_____
_____
_____
_____
_____

KEY VERSES

PRAYER

_____
_____
_____
_____
_____
_____
_____
_____
_____
_____
_____
_____
_____
_____
_____
_____
_____

KEY POINTS

APPLICATION

Prayer journal

DATE

TODAY'S PASSAGE　　　PREACHER　　　SERMON TOPIC

NOTES

KEY VERSES

PRAYER

KEY POINTS

APPLICATION

Prayer journal

DATE

TODAY'S PASSAGE   PREACHER   SERMON TOPIC

NOTES

KEY VERSES

PRAYER

KEY POINTS

APPLICATION

"The LORD will open the heavens, the storehouse of his bounty, to send rain on your land in season and to bless all the work of your hands. You will lend to many nations but will borrow from none." - Deuteronomy 28:12

Monthly Prayer List

Prayer	Answered

Prayer journal

DATE

TODAY'S PASSAGE   PREACHER   SERMON TOPIC

NOTES

KEY VERSES

PRAYER

KEY POINTS

APPLICATION

Prayer journal

DATE _____

TODAY'S PASSAGE   PREACHER   SERMON TOPIC

NOTES

| KEY VERSES |

PRAYER

| KEY POINTS |

| APPLICATION |

Prayer journal

DATE

TODAY'S PASSAGE　　　PREACHER　　　SERMON TOPIC

NOTES

KEY VERSES

PRAYER

KEY POINTS

APPLICATION

Prayer journal

DATE

TODAY'S PASSAGE   PREACHER   SERMON TOPIC

NOTES

KEY VERSES

PRAYER

KEY POINTS

APPLICATION

Prayer journal

DATE

TODAY'S PASSAGE   PREACHER   SERMON TOPIC

NOTES

KEY VERSES

PRAYER

KEY POINTS

APPLICATION

"I praise you because I am fearfully and wonderfully made; your works are wonderful, I know that full well." - Psalm 139:14

Prayer List

Prayer	Answered

"She is clothed with strength and dignity; she can laugh at the days to come." - Proverbs 31:25

www.ingramcontent.com/pod-product-compliance
Lightning Source LLC
Chambersburg PA
CBHW042125100526
44587CB00026B/4178